THE
GHOST RIDER
AND I

THE
GHOST RIDER
AND I

THE AUTOBIOGRAPHY OF PATRICK JOSEPH (JOE) WHITE,
IRISH CYCLING LEGEND AND WORLD RECORD HOLDER

carrowmore.ie

This edition first published 2020
Published in Ireland by Carrowmore Publishing

Carrrowmore
6-9 City Quay
Dublin 2
www.carrowmore.ie
info@carrowmore.ie

First Edition

ISBN: 978-1-9993234-6-2

Printed in Ireland*

Design by www.carrowmore.ie

To my wife Katheen (RIP), who was always there for me, and was inspirational in encouraging me; to my family, Catherine, Maria, Paul and Patricia; to my sister Mary Ann; to all my relations, grandchildren and great grandchildren.

To my father and mother (RIP), wonderful parents; to my brothers John and Michael (RIP); to Brendan and Carmel (An Siopa Dubh), thank you for your kindness to me; to the people of Bracaragh, Castlecove, Caherdaniel.

I trust that I have done you proud.

CONTENTS

Introduction   11

Chapter 1
The Beginning   14

Chapter 2
My First Race   18

Chapter 3
Leinster 25 Miles TT Championship   22

Chapter 4
All-Ireland Junior Championship   25

Chapter 5
25-Mile All-Ireland Championship   29

Chapter 6
Training for Racing   31

Chapter 7
A New Racing Bicycle   33

Chapter 8
Round the Houses, Cork City   34

Chapter 9
3-Mile Track Championship of Ireland   37

Chapter 10
100-Mile Time Trial Championship of Ireland 1952   39

Chapter 11
Inter-County All-Ireland Championship 1952   42

Chapter 12
Tóstal Races 1952/1953   43

Chapter 13
50-Mile Time Trial Championship of Ireland 1952   45

Chapter 14
Training for the 1953 Racing Season   47

Chapter 15
Ring of Kerry Cycle Race 1953   49

Chapter 16
100-Mile Time Trial Championship of Ireland 1953   53

Chapter 17
50-Mile TT All-Ireland Championship 1954   57

Chapter 18
All-Army Road Cycling Championship   60

Chapter 19
All-Army 3-Mile Track Championship 1954   62

Chapter 20
100-Mile Time Trial Championship of Ireland 1954   64

Chapter 21
The Rás 1954: Eight-Day Race Around Ireland   69

Chapter 22
The First Stage of the Rás: Dublin to Wexford   71

Chapter 23
The Second Stage of the Rás: Wexford to Cork   73

Chapter 24
The Third Stage of the Rás: Cork to Tralee   75

Chapter 25
The Fourth Stage of the Rás: Tralee to Ennis   77

Chapter 26
The Fifth Stage of the Rás: Ennis to Galway   79

Chapter 27
Achievements   81

Chapter 28
That 100-Mile Time Trial World Record   83

Chapter 29
Related Events   85

Chapter 30
The Iron Man   87

Conclusion   89

Postscript
Who was the Ghost Rider?   92

INTRODUCTION

Patrick Joseph White was born in Bracaragh, Castlecove, Co. Kerry, in 1931. He was the second eldest of four children and had two brothers and one sister.

His eldest brother, John, emigrated to the USA and was conscripted into the American Marines. He was wounded, taken prisoner and died in captivity during the Korean War in the 1950s. He was awarded the Purple Heart. May he rest in peace.

Joseph's younger brother, Michael, went to England and his sister, Mary Ann, went to the USA.

Their mother died when Joseph was 13 years old. Consequently, life became a struggle for the family.

Attending school in Caherdaniel was a challenge as the family home was 3 miles from the school building. Joseph started school at the age of 4 and walked to school without any footwear for several years. The first pair of shoes he received were hand-me-downs from his eldest brother John and had been re-soled and repaired several times (Tiobhins).

Joseph fondly remembers how pupils would bring the sod of turf to school to boil water, make cocoa and heat the classrooms. The teacher always stood in front of the fire. Very little heat would be emitted into the classroom, so the pupils had to keep their coats on in winter time.

The family's staple diet consisted of mackerel and herring, potatoes and plenty of buttermilk. When there was no fish, a dish of potatoes and milk, known as "dip", was the order of the day: the potatoes would be dipped into the milk and eaten with a pinch of salt. Meat was only eaten at Christmas, if they could afford it.

The family made its income rearing turkeys for sale at Christmas, selling milk to the creamery and selling the odd cow. The money was used to buy essentials, like clothing, flour for making bread and so on.

When Joseph finished national school, he attended the technical school in Waterville, but he had to leave after two years because the family did not have enough money. He hoped to become a carpenter as carpentry was in the family. His father was a fisherman and small farmer and always did his best for the family.

The primary sport in Kerry was football. The local club was Derrynane GAA and everything in the community revolved around GAA. Joseph also was handy at the hop-step-jump, a tradition in South Kerry.

Looking back now, it was a wonderful, happy life. There were no millionaires around – everybody was at the same level.

Storytelling was another one of Joseph's interests. Some of the stories that were told back then would frighten the life out of you, such as tales of the banshee, people rising up from the grave, strange noises and so on. Crossroad dancing was also very popular; although, the local priest always said in his sermons that such dances were not in the best interest of the locals as the "carry-on" was unacceptable. Those dances would go on until the small hours of the morning, so maybe he had a point.

Joseph went to Dublin for work as there was no work around Bracaragh. He worked in an electrical shop for a year and a half. However, the wages were low, so he decided to the army Air Corps to study aeronautical engineering. This was the beginning of an extraordinary period in his life.

During his training, he took up cycle racing. He went on to win many all-Ireland titles and set a world record in 1954.

When he had completed his engineering training, he worked for Aer Lingus. He went on to gain a diploma in Aeronautical Engineering and joined the civil service as an Aeronautical Inspector. He rose through the ranks of the civil service and ultimately became the Chief Aeronautical Inspector (in Irish Aviation) of the Regulatory Department (the highest technical position). He represented Ireland at many aviation conferences, lectured in Limerick University, Kevin Street and Bolton Street Colleges and, upon retiring, worked for the European Union.

Chapter 1
The Beginning

Growing up in Bracaragh, Co. Kerry, I used to cycle from our family home to Ballybog, where we cut turf and harvested it for the fire. Turf fires were the only means of cooking meals, boiling water and keeping the house warm in the winter. In those days, there was no electricity, central heating or cooking stoves.

Travelling to and from the bog, I used to cycle under the crossbar. I wasn't tall enough to sit on the saddle, but the cycling made me fit and I have retained a high level of fitness to this day.

There was an annual sports day that was held in a field near An Siopa Dubh. It was a great day out. The locals competed in the 100 yards, the half-mile, the one-mile, the high jump, hop-step-jump, cycle racing and tug of war.

The events were managed by the locals and there were always arguments about who had won what and the distances involved. Winners were considered local heroes. I competed in a cycling event, cycling under the crossbar. I was up against a guy named Galvin from Sneem, among others. Galvin was a renowned cycle racer. His bicycle had turned-down handlebars and cane wheels – all the signs of a racer. He looked a treat, but us locals took him on. We would not let our area down.

The starter lined us up. He was hard to hear because his voice was gone from shouting all day. As a result, several locals took off before the official start call. It was a 3-mile race around the field, each lap of which was equal to a quarter of a mile (give or take).

No sooner had the race started than there was a "pile-up", with Galvin in the middle. Some choice language was used, I can tell you. Bicycles were knotted together and there was a bit of blood, but nothing serious.

The guys who jumped the gun were way up front, but when Galvin extracted himself from the pile-up, he took off in pursuit. I got up and started to ride again. Galvin was far ahead. He succeeded in lapping the lot of us and there was confusion about how many laps he had completed and, for that matter, how many laps anyone had completed.

The race was stopped and Galvin was declared the winner. But there was an objection. It was pointed out by some local genius that Galvin had only completed 2½ miles (ten laps). There followed about 20 minutes of heated argument, with some calling for Galvin to be suspended, but on the toss of a coin, Galvin was declared the winner. To this day, the locals maintain that a local had in fact won (not me – I was lapped several times). The Galvin in question was John Galvin from Sneem – he had won many big races and had been awarded a Munster medal.

Whilst I was serving in the Air Corps, part of my training was keeping fit, an area in which I excelled. I made full use of the gym facilities. I was also involved in track-and-field events and played a lot of GAA with the Air Corps.

One day, I went to Dublin city and was rambling around when I came upon a bicycle shop called Rutland Cycles on North Frederick Street. The racing bicycles displayed in the window caught my eye. I was entranced. I went in and met the owner, Jack Fagan, for the first time. He seemed like a nice man. He asked me if I'd ever competed in a race.

"Yes," I said. "When I was a young man, I rode against John Galvin of Sneem."

He said, "Did you win?"

"No," I said, "he lapped me about six times. It was a three-miler."

Before I left the shop, I had purchased a second-hand tourer (not a racer) and agreed to buy it on the never-never.

It had high pressures, dropped handlebars and a three-gear sprocket. It was on the heavy side, but it was a start – and what a start it was. I was out on it every chance I got. At first, I was covering only about 10 miles. After six months, I was covering around 20 miles. This was in 1950.

I was also getting cheeky. Whilst out for a cycle, I used to latch onto other cyclists or groups and try to keep up with them. I was able to do this for a while, but when they sped up, I fell behind. Why? Because the bicycle was too heavy and not fit for racing. I decided to train harder over the winter of 1950 and into 1951 and I read a lot of cycling books. I went back to Rutland Cycles and got a lighter bike, a second-hand Peugeot racer, again on the never-never. This bicycle had five sprockets and two chain wheels. I embarked on long-distance cycles on my own. By the end of 1951, I was doing 100 miles solo every weekend and about another 100 miles during the week. That amounts to roughly 10,000 miles a year.

It was tough, but I loved it. When I wanted to stop, a cyclist would appear about 50 yards ahead of me. I would try to catch up with him, but I never could. He was always ahead of me and made me cycle harder. As soon as I got going again, he would disappear.

These visions of a cyclist up ahead made me worry about my health. Maybe the cycling was getting to my brain. I didn't tell anyone. That guy played a big part in my future as a cyclist.

During the winter of 1951, I put everything into training. There was no smoking, no dancing, early bedtimes, plenty of miles and a proper diet. Concentration was vital.

Chapter 2
My First Race

All the training, all the hours and the sweat, all the sacrifices, the hundreds of miles put in on the road, the torture on the hills – would it pay off?

My first race was on a Sunday morning on the Naas Road, a competitor-paced (CP) race of approximately 45 miles. The race started near Clondalkin and travelled to Naas and back.

The competitors consisted of:

Novices: Those who had never won anything. I was part of this group, which would start about 5 minutes before the next group.

Intermediates: Those who had won races other than championships or other graded races. Those in this group would start 5 minutes before the next group. There were a couple of talented riders in this group that were ready to move up in class to senior status.

Scratch men: These were the best racers. They had trophies to show for their efforts and were the group that everyone wanted to be associated with.

As I was a beginner and didn't know about the differences between groups or anyone at the event, when I arrived I mingled with one of the groups, not realising that I was mingling with the scratch men.

"Which group are you?" one of them asked me.

"I don't know," I said,

"Did you ever win anything?"

"No," I replied.

"Well, your bunch is over there, the Novices."

Over I went to the novices. My God, the smell of embrocation would knock you down. My new bike attracted a lot of attention.

"What club do you belong to?"

"The Air Corps," I said.

"Did you race before?"

"No, I did not."

"Novices over here!" the starter shouted.

I was shaking with nervousness. As the bunch lined up, I positioned myself to the rear.

"Go!" the starter shouted.

My God, this bunch of novices took off like mad men. There was no system. It was every man for himself. I stayed at the back. The other cyclists did not know me or my form.

I settled down as the pace eased, because nobody wanted to work too hard – great, I could cope easily, but I realised that if this group couldn't organise itself, it would be overtaken by the second group. I kept looking back. After about 5 miles, I spotted the second group approaching us at speed. I detached myself from the novices by easing back and giving myself enough space to pick up speed so I could latch onto the group coming up behind us. As the second group was passing the novices, I got in at the rear and stayed there until all hell broke loose.

Someone shouted, "The scratch men are coming up!"

Some riders tried to stay clear, but couldn't. The scratch men were well organised. Now that we had to turn for home, all of the novices had fallen behind, except me. I stayed at the back. I could cope with the pace, but I sensed that I was being noticed at the rear of the pack. Riders kept looking back, probably thinking, "Who in hell is that fellow hanging in behind?" I don't think I worried them too much.

As we were approaching Clondalkin and the finish line, the pace was tough. Some riders dropped out, but I hung in there. With 2 miles to go, one rider attacked and got away. There was only one rider that made an effort to go after him. Without thinking, I attacked and opened a gap. No one chased me down. I think the other cyclists were in shock. They were fighting amongst themselves. I got clear.

Suddenly, I saw this image of a cyclist on a bike in front of me, coaxing me to put in more effort. I closed in on the lone rider who had got away initially. He didn't realise that I was closing in on him fast. When I got within about 10 yards of him, I jumped on the pedals, taking him by surprise and winning easily.

It was my first big win and it came as a complete surprise. The next day a piece on the sports page read:

Novice Rider wins G.P.
A young Kerryman riding his first race beat the cream of Irish Cycling. Watch out for this cyclist in future races, his name is Paddy White.

After that race, I received numerous offers to join clubs, but I declined. I was comfortable with where I was.

The Air Corps was delighted with my win. The victory had been the result of all the hard work I had put in and the way the Air Corps had looked after me.

I had dinner back in Baldonnel and, an hour later, I was out on the road again, putting in more miles. I went to bed early that night, happy with the win. Yes, it was the beginning.

CHAPTER 3
LEINSTER 25-MILE
TT CHAMPIONSHIP

That race, the 45-mile CP, did me a lot of good. My confidence was high, but I kept my head and did not lose the run of myself. I put the victory down to luck, but would my luck last? When I was developing my time-trial technique, I had issues pacing myself and judging distance over 25 miles, as my training was over 100 miles, which very different to 25 miles.

A time trial is a race against the clock. If you want to win or get placed, you have to ride hard. There is no place to hide, as in a massed start. Time trialling is one of the toughest sports. After winning the 45-mile CP, I competed in a few other races without any success, but when it came to championships, I had a different outlook: my concentration was high, my approach was good and I was able to read other competitors.

This 25 TT was my first, so it would be a marker for the future. It was held on the Navan Road, outside Dublin city, an out-and-home route. I arrived early and tried to relax, as I had butterflies in my stomach and was feeling a bit nervous. As a novice, I would be starting early. The favourites would be the last to start. There would be 1 minute between starts. I was fifth to start. I did not know those in front of me or their form.

It was me versus the clock, rather than any individual, so concentration was vital. After about 5 miles, I had caught up with and passed a couple of those who had started before me and although this gave me some satisfaction, I was aware that the big boys were coming up behind me. After about 10 miles, I was out in front and no rider had caught up with me yet. So I thought I was doing fairly well and pushing a bit hard. I was not yet at the halfway mark of 12.5 miles.

When I turned for home, I could see the other competitors on their way to the halfway mark, but I noted that there were big gaps between riders. It was hard to judge what the positions were, but it looked as if those who had started last were catching up with those who had started before them. "To hell with it," I said to myself, "let's go." So, I put everything into the last half and headed for the finish. Having passed the finish line, I kept going for a while, easing my pace to cool off. When I made my way back, everyone was looking at me. Why? Because my time was 1 hour and 30 seconds. Unbelievable!

However, there were still some very good, experienced riders who had yet to finish, including Tony Lavin from Cork, a great TT man; John Lackey from Longford; Bernie O'Brien from Kildare; Phil Clarke from Dublin and others.

When the race was over, the results were announced:

1st	Dennis O'Connor, Dublin	1 hour 25 seconds
2nd	Paddy White, Kerry	1 hour 30 seconds
3rd	John Lackey Longford	1 hour 2 minutes

Dennis O'Connor ("Young O'Connor", I called him) was younger than I was. He rode an exceptional race and would go on to prove that he was no pushover. He won many races (MS), including championships. Dennis and I were the youngest in the race and he had beaten me, fair and square. We controlled the 25-mile TT races. I beat him as many times as he beat me. We became friends and respected each other. I was delighted that I had come second, but I knew that I could have won if only I had more experience. Next time it would be different. From that day until I finished racing, I won eight 25-mile TT races, one of which was an all-Ireland competition.

CHAPTER 4
ALL-IRELAND JUNIOR CHAMPIONSHIP

I had placed second in the Leinster 25-Mile TT Champion-ship. I had won my first race and many other races, though I lost a good few as well. However, the junior championship race was for an all-Ireland medal, so it had to be taken very seriously. I trained very hard and concentrated on the race to the exclusion of all else. Naturally, every rider wanted to win, including me. My name, Paddy White, had spread through the clubs and I could hear the remarks that were made when I ar-rived at the start of races:

"There's White there. Over in the corner."

"That's not Whit e..."

"It is, I tell you."

"He shouldn't be here, isn't he a senior rider?"

"No, he is qualified as he hasn't won an all-Ireland Senior

Championship yet."

"Didn't he win the GP?"

"Yes, he did, but it was GP, not a scratch race."

"Keep an eye on him, don't let him dictate."

"Okay ..."

I always made sure that my racing bike was clean and oiled and that the tyre pressure was right, the brakes in good shape and the saddle and handlebars secure. But I also made sure I could twist them, so that in the event of a crash, I could turn them.

Leaving Baldonnel early on a Saturday, I cycled through Ballyboughal and on to Naul village, where the race would start at around 6 p.m. I stayed out of the way until just before the start and didn't make myself known. Someone recognised me and word spread like wildfire. Heads started turning my way. I kept cool and pretended that I was unaware of the comments being made. Some of the comments weren't very nice. But I suppose I had earned a reputation as an aggressive rider who took no prisoners. I was learning cycle racing very fast. A young cyclist told me that he had been advised to "keep away from White, because if you don't, he will kill you". That comment made my day.

The race started on level ground. Around fifty riders were taking part. The usual attacks were made, but they didn't come to much and the riders were hauled in very quickly. It was a dangerous race as some inexperienced riders were causing trouble within the pack. They were all over the place, so the only answer was to get rid of them. I made my way to the front and set a steady pace for a while, then I put on pressure, which was too much for these inexperienced riders. Most of them fell behind. The race settled down until we came to a steep hill. Two guys attacked. I remained calm. They opened a gap. I watched it to make sure it didn't get too big. The rest of the bunch stayed together, but I realised that most of the riders expected me to chase down the two guys up front. This made me happy, but I wasn't going to show my hand. I stayed where I was. This got to some of the other riders. They wanted the two in front to be hauled in. They attacked to catch the two riders. Four got away. They started to work together and increased the gap. I started to worry, but realised that if I attacked on the level, the rest of the pack would latch on to my wheel, but no one would come up and help. My time would come. The hill – that was the answer. I would crucify them on the hill. They were all watching me. I eased back to the rear of the bunch. The hill was not too far away.

Get ready for it. I set the pace. It was a short sprint and I started to climb. I knew that I was creating havoc behind me. I knew from the cursing and bad language that a lot of the pack couldn't keep up with me. I got over the top of the hill, looked back and noted that only about ten had survived my attack. By attacking so hard on the hill, I had also closed the gap between myself and the guys that had broken away earlier. I was determined to maintain that gap. The hill had to be climbed twice more. I knew that the guys up front were getting worried, because they could see a group not too far back. In that group was Paddy White.

Everything was going well. The guys with me realised that they couldn't get rid of me and they were right. I was dominating them, dictating to them, marshalling them, making them work to maintain the gap. My group of eleven climbed the hill at a steady pace, staying together and keeping the gap. To ensure I had a chance, I had to close the gap before the next climb, so I organised my comrades to increase their speed. They did their best. I had plenty to spare. The hill would lead me to glory or bust.

At the beginning of the final climb, there was a gap of only a few yards between us and the four in front. I attacked, increasing the pressure as I climbed, dropping everyone and opening a big gap. I was away on my own. I started to time trial as best I could, as a result of which I gained ground all the way to the finish line. What a race. I had won an all-Ireland championship.

One of the competitors said to me, "Only for I got a puncture on the hill, you wouldn't have won."

I smiled.

CHAPTER 5
25-MILE ALL-IRELAND
CHAMPIONSHIP

I had had a lot of success during my first year, so I entered the 25-mile All-Ireland Championship, which would be held on a course that was well known to me: the Navan Road.

On Sunday morning, I went to church in Inchicore. I stayed at the back of the church with the bicycle. The racing shoes I was wearing had a steel piece at the base of the foot and would make a lot of noise if I walked up the church – clip-clop, clip-clop. Imagine. And me all togged out in my cycling gear.

Afterwards, I went into a cake shop. I drank a pint of milk and devoured a sugary doughnut, then cycled to the start. The race would begin at 10 a.m. The smell of embrocation was overpowering. I went for a short spin to keep supple and concentrate. I was in good shape and determined to beat the guys who had already put one across on me. As I started out, I felt strong and determined, but I had learnt a lot about time trialling: I had to pace myself and save something for the last 5 miles, which is when the 25 is won or lost. I could have gone a few miles per hour faster, but I kept repeating to myself, "No, no, no, hold it." When I got to the turn, I had already caught up with many riders, some of whom had recently beaten me in 25 TTs. I was fiercely determined and still in control of my speed.

As I was getting closer to the finish, I rode as hard as I could. I flew past rider after rider over the last 5 miles, crossed the line and won the 25-Mile All-Ireland Championship.

My time was 1 hour and 14 seconds.

Here I must highlight that although I was a renowned in cycling circles in Leinster, Ulster and Connaught, I wasn't known in Kerry, the place of my birth.

There are many reasons for this. Publicity was poor in those days and the name Paddy White would not have been recognised in Kerry at that time, because I was known at home as Joseph White.

CHAPTER 6
TRAINING FOR RACING

Throughout 1951, I put my heart and soul into training. I avoided smoking, dances and the cinema and made sure that I got at least 8 hours sleep every night. First thing every morning, I did about twenty dips and presses and a run of about 2 miles before breakfast, which consisted of porridge, brown bread and jam, and lots of milk. At dinner, I had either fish or chicken, with lots of vegetables, such carrots, parsnips and cabbage. Three times a week, I had a lean steak, which I ate rare.

Working in the gym was special, as I had the use of weights, an indoor track and rollers. Many's the hour I spent there, sometimes becoming so involved that I lost track of time. If the weekends were fine, I would be out on the road putting in the miles, on the flat and mountain climbing.

Here I must acknowledge the help I received from Air Corps personnel. Firstly, Colonel Cathan, who had been an Irish High

Jump Champion in his youth, took a special interest in me and ensured that I was looked after. Brigadier General Gerry O'Connor, a special friend, a great Kerryman and a fantastic sportsman, also showed an interest in me. I was given time off duties to facilitate my training, I had medical back-up and I had a cook to ensure that I had my meals.

On Sundays, weather permitting, I cycled up to 100 miles and during the week, I would cycle around 400 miles. As I improved my cycling fitness, this increased to 500 miles per week – or approximately 25,000 miles per year. I was probably the only cyclist in Ireland who put in this much effort during training.

I decided that if I was going to be a racer, I had to have a real racing machine, so I went into Rutland and discussed my situation with Jack Fagan. He asked me what I wanted and I told him that I wanted the best.

"The best," he said, "will cost you around £100.00."

I thought about it for a while and then said, "Get me the best, a bicycle fit for road and grass track."

Jack said, "There is a bicycle called a Hill Special, named after a famous British racer and it will cost around £70."

"I'll take it."

I had saved some money, plus I would also be given money from the army to support my racing efforts. The rest I would pay on the never-never. It was a deal. The bike would be available in two weeks.

Jack's advice was: "Keep the bike you have and use it for the winter training. Your new bike is only for racing."

Jack also told me that there had been a fellow in the shop a few days previously who had said, "White is a professional, he is training every day."

I was ready to start.

CHAPTER 7
A NEW RACING BICYCLE

The bicycle arrived. What a beauty. It was chrome-plated and weighed around 19 lb. Jack Fagan advised me to take it easy and get used to the bike. It had one chain wheel and five gear sprockets. I had to get a new pair of cycling shoes, new togs and a jersey. My jersey was the one the Air Corps touring team used. It was red with a sash across the front. When I got into my racing outfit and cycled past a glass window, I used to look at myself and think, "You look the real thing."

It took me a while to get used to the bike and I made a lot of adjustments until I felt happy with it. During the spring of 1952, I put in a final session of training in preparation for the racing season.

CHAPTER 8
ROUND THE HOUSES, CORK CITY

A letter arrived for me one day from George Harding of Harding Cycles, Cork, who invited me to participate in a round-the-houses race sponsored by Harding Cycles. I hadn't raced on the road in Cork previously, but I decided to take part nonetheless. I didn't know that Mr Harding had issued invitations to racers from Northern Ireland, Wales, France, Scotland, as well as many of the top Irish riders. It was a big event with lots of prizes and awards, including such titles as King of the Hills and Most Aggressive Rider.

When I arrived at the start, I was greeted with a chorus of boos from the Cork supporters there to support their own riders. I was getting used to that kind of welcome, especially when I rode on the grass track. The Cork supporters told me to go home, that Cork racers would sort me out. I remained focused on the race. I had cycled the course early that morning and made a plan. There was a section that included a steep climb and an S-bend near the top. Ideal. I concluded that that was where the race could be won or lost. After the climb, it was downhill, with a few dangerous bends, and on to a straight road towards the finish.

The race started with all the novices up front, fighting for position. They did not realise the danger up ahead. The riders would have to make a sharp left turn onto a bridge over a river. Anyone with any experience would know that it would be necessary to approach this bridge at a slow pace. But these mad, young riders tore into it and a few didn't make it, bringing down other riders with them, including a couple of experienced riders, who should have known better. Later, I found that there had been no serious injuries, just hurt pride.

The pace was reasonable until we came to the climb, when an almighty attack was staged. I don't know who started it, but it split the bunch into several units. I was caught in the third bunch – not too bad, but there was a gap to be aware of. As long as I could see the leading group, I was happy enough.

The race carried on for about eight laps (40 miles). It was getting serious. With only about half the riders left, the hill was taking its toll, but I applied some pressure and succeeded in joining the second group. The first group were in trouble – I knew because they kept looking back. I was also aware that those around me were not working; they were just sitting in. Well, I was not going to let them use me, so on the next lap I started to go harder and harder, stringing them out. They could not keep up with me. I was on fire. I went up the hill and caught up with the first bunch. Panic. They did not know what was coming next.

I looked around and said to myself, "There have to be sprinters in this bunch and I can't let them be there at the finish." I calculated that I would have the last two climbs to sort them out. During the second last lap, I started the climb normally and slowly increased the pressure. I did not look back, but sensed that only a few were following. Who were they? A quick look back. I didn't recognise any of them. What would I do now? Wait for the last S-bend – that's what I'd do. During the last lap, I kept up the pressure, giving no one a chance to relax and, as I had anticipated, a couple attacked at the start of the climb. I got in behind them and let them at it.

"Up the Kingdom!" someone shouted.

The crowd was out on the road.

"Come on White! Go White!"

It was dangerous. The crowd was almost blocking our pathway. I got a good few slaps on the back from well-wishers (I hope). Now that all the Cork riders were out, the Cork supporters began to cheer me on, which was hard to believe.

My plan was to stay close until halfway up the hill, when I would attack. I almost sprinted for the S-bend, opened a gap and sped down the hill without any regard for my safety. When I got to level ground, I looked around. I was clear to ride as I had never ridden before to win what I consider one of the greatest victories of my cycling career.

When I stopped and got off the bike, I was surrounded by well-wishers – mostly Cork people, for a change. Three hours previously, they had told me to go home, but I know from my experiences of many other races in Cork that they didn't mean it – in fairness to them, Cork people are good sportspeople.

I was presented with a beautiful cup, a medal for being King of the Hills and a plaque for being the Most Aggressive Rider. It had been great day's racing.

CHAPTER 9
3-MILE TRACK
CHAMPIONSHIP OF IRELAND

Cork City Sports was one of the biggest events (covering field and track) held in the Republic of Ireland. In 1952, this event included competitions between international military states: the USA, France, Spain, Norway and Ireland. I was selected to represent the Irish army in a three-mile track cycling event, which I won. And with wins by Mick Byrne (Irish Mile Champion), Dessie McConvill (Irish 200-yards champion), the Irish team (all Air Corps) was the overall winning team.

Whilst we were hanging around, some track events were taking place. The three-mile championship of Ireland would take place in half an hour. Would I take part in it? I wasn't that anxious because the top trackmen were there: O'Reilly, Bard and Mannion, to name but a few. I didn't stand a chance against those men. When the time came, I took my bike to the start line and asked the stewards if I could compete.

"Yes," they said. "What is your name?"

"White," I told them.

"Have you ever won a track race before?"

"Yes," I said, "about an hour ago."

"Oh, that. Get in at the back."

I started at the back and stayed there for the first couple of laps until the pack was drawn out by a rider who cycled to the front and put on the pressure. A few riders were slipping behind because of the pace being set at the front. We had covered 1 mile and I was still at the rear. Nobody took any notice of me. I wasn't considered a serious competitor. Some choice language was used in the pack. Everyone was trying to keep their position. I stayed out of it. This was all new to me. I wasn't a track man. I was a time triallist and a mass-start road man. After 2 miles, I was still there, but it was then that the pace increased and the attacks began. I had to hang on. With two laps to go, everyone was watching each other, the pace was now down and the sprinters were moving up towards the front.

Without any plan or forethought, I sprinted past them and opened a gap. The bunch wasn't worried – sure, that fellow hasn't a clue, he won't last long. But I did and with one lap to go I was getting farther and farther away. I won by around 100 yards. I hardly realised what I had done. It was because of my high level of fitness that I had won the 3-mile track championship of Ireland, thus becoming the first Kerryman to win an all-Ireland on the track.

Chapter 10
100-Mile Time Trial
Championship of Ireland
1952

This was my first big test. I had trained solo for many months on the roads and hills of Leinster and had kept to a rigid fitness schedule. I was very much looking forward to this race. It should be noted that I was new to bicycle racing (sure, I had just started).

The race was held on the Navan Road, outside Dublin, so I had to cycle about 15 miles to get there, which was a good warm-up.

There was a stiff wind and heavy rain during the race. The conditions weren't particularly comfortable for any of the competitors. The lack of mudguards only made the experience worse as the wheels sprayed up rainwater from the front and rear.

I arrived at the start in good time. I hardly knew most of the competitors or, more importantly, their form, which was just as well. However, I had three bottles of liquid and enough liver to sustain me for the duration of the race, which would likely take over 4 hours. I had trained on my own and was comfortable cycling long distances, but now there was an all-Ireland at stake. I had to keep this in mind and concentrate. Before the start, I felt a little jittery, but as soon as I got the GO!, I settled down to a steady pace. I knew that there was a long way to go.

Several riders passed me at speed, but I remained focused on my own calculations. Yes, it was tough, but I was in it now and I had to finish.

Everything was going well for the first 50 miles. I was putting on more pressure and managed to reel in those that had already passed me early on. It was a great feeling, even though I was drenched. I had no mechanical defects as yet and I was feeling very relaxed. No other rider passed me until there about 25 miles to go. My right leg seized up with an almighty cramp in the calf. I fell off the bike into the ditch. It took a while to loosen my right strap and release my leg. I was in terrible pain as I had hit my shoulder on the road when I fell. I thought I was finished. I got up and started to slowly ease out the cramp. Some blood was coming from where my left elbow had hit the road.

I now started to run slowly, checking the bike for damage, but it was okay. Several riders passed me. I was in dreamland. I slowly recovered to settle down into my time-trial rhythm. I started to put on pressure. I saw this cyclist up front, waving me on. I tried to catch him, but I couldn't, no matter how hard I tried. I was cycling very fast in order to catch up with this rider. He made me ride beyond my capability at that stage of the race. Suddenly, he was gone. I was confused – had I been seeing things? But I remembered having seen this guy out in front of me on a few occasions when I was out training. Try as I might, I could never catch up with him.

There it was. I was approaching the finish line. I sprinted and crossed the line, exhausted, drenched and disappointed. I picked up my tracksuit and went home. A week later, at a National Athletic and Cycling Association (NCA) meeting, I was informed that I had won a silver medal for second place, with a time of 4 hours and 8 minutes. The winner's time had been 4 hours, 7 minutes and 43 seconds. A difference of only 17 seconds!

I was happy with silver, but I had to find out about that cramp. I went to see a doctor and he prescribed some tablets and told me to take one before any long-distance race or when I was travelling long distances during training.

The problem, he told me, was a lack of salt!

CHAPTER 11
INTER-COUNTY ALL-IRELAND
CHAMPIONSHIP 1952

The Inter-County All-Ireland Team Championship took place at the end of the racing season. Each team consisted of three riders. The winners were the team with the best total time and the individual with the best time.

I often waited to see if any other Kerry riders would show up, but none ever did. As I was a highly rated time triallist, the Dublin team asked me to join them, which I did. We went on to win the team championship of Ireland. It was a very good Dublin team and we had lots of time to spare compared to any other team. About ten took part. A Cork man beat me in the individual competition by a number of seconds.

However, I was on the winning team and so I won a medal, an all-Ireland, inter-county team medal. I won three such medals in total over the years.

CHAPTER 12
TÓSTAL RACES
1952/1953

I competed in four Tóstal races during 1952-1953. The first was held in Dublin on a Sunday morning and was set to start at around 10 a.m. However, another race was being promoted by Cumann Rothaíochta na hÉireann (CRE) and didn't finish until 10:30 a.m. My NCA race was delayed until the CRE race had finished.

The finish for both races was a straight stretch of road, but as a result of the politics involved in the event, the NCA organisers shifted the finish of their race forward around a turn. This was not made known to most riders, although I have no doubt in my mind that some NCA competitors were made aware of the change.

Having competed three laps, I turned onto the final straight. I noted a large crowd at the original finish, attacked and went clear. I opened up a big gap and sprinted for the (original) finish. I got off the bike, as did about 90 per cent of the other riders, but there were a few who kept going around the bend to finish at the new finishing line. Protesting made little difference. The NCA judges had the final say. Yes, politics did play a part. There was great rivalry between the CRE and the NCA.

I then rode in three other Tóstal races and won all three.

CHAPTER 13
50-MILE TIME TRIAL
CHAMPIONSHIP OF IRELAND
1952

This race was held on the out-and-home course on the Navan Road. I had six weeks to prepare. I rode the course several times, clocking about 2 hours 10 minutes. This race had been won with a best time of 2 hours 12 minutes, so I had a chance.

As I trained on the roads and mountain, I continued seeing a friendly rider up ahead that I could never catch up with – my "Ghost Rider". He drew the best out of me, especially in time trials.

On the day of the race, I was about the twentieth rider to go. A time of 2 minutes separated each rider. I settled down and rode comfortably, catching up with some riders who had started before me. All was going well until I had travelled about 10 miles. I didn't feel well and had to get of my bicycle to vomit.

"What is this?" I asked myself. "This never happened before."

I had prepared in the same way I had for other races.

I was losing time. I got back on the bike. My legs were very weak and it took a while before I recovered fully and got back to riding strongly. I was beaten by 20 seconds and took second place. I was upset, even though I had won a silver medal.

I pressed on and got ready for my next big race.

The time for the 50 miles was 2 hours, 1 minute and 45 seconds.

Chapter 14
Training for the 1953 Racing Season

Since I started training in 1951-1952, my schedule had grown increasingly challenging: more miles on the road, more hill climbing, more time in the gym. Yes, it was tough, but I had to do it to maintain fitness. My achievements in 1952 put me up there with the top riders and I had to commit to a very high standard to maintain my status.

Time trialling is a very hard form of competition. It is considered to be second only to rowing. Pacing oneself is vital. Judgement over a long or short distance is an art that must be developed over time. During such races, you see some riders starting at high speed, whereas others don't ride so fast initially, but as the race progresses, they take control and put in the final miles at maximum speed.

Covering over 100 miles during training was normal for

me and I usually trained solo. This built up my endurance and concentration, both of which were invaluable in competitive races. Of course, I also had the assistance of the Ghost Rider.

Early in 1953, I was anxious to start racing. My plan was to ride the 100, the 50, plus a few massed-start and trial races.

P.J. White, All-Ireland Cycling Champion, 1952, 1953, 1954.

1954 Rás, prior to start at GPO.

Air Corps cross-country team, 1956, trained by Corp. Sgt White.

Above: All-round Road All-Ireland Championship, Cork 1953 Winner. Tom Lavin (Cork) 2nd on my right.

Right: Certificate from Ring of Kerry Charity Cycle.

12

RING OF KERRY
VOLUNTARY CYCLE

This is to certify that

P. J. White

cycled around the Ring of Kerry
on

30 - 7 - 1994

signed .... organizer

witnessed .... event secretary

Above: An Siopa Dubh, Castlecove - focal point for get together.

Below: Army Cycling Team.

Above: Seine Boat Racing: a popular sport in Kerry. My father is 3rd from the right and everyone on the boat is related. This was at the Sneem Regatta and they won on the day.

Below: Finish of the Rás in Kildara. Winner.

Above left: The author's brother, John White. He was awarded the Purple Heart during the Korean War. He was captured and died in 1952.
Above right: The author's brother, Michael White.
Below: The author and family.

Cathleen and Joseph.

The author with his sister, Mary Ann.

Above:: Medal collection.

Below: Trophy collection.

Above: Cork Round The Houses, Winner. George Harding trophy presentation.

Below: Immortalised in stone outside An Siopa Dubh, Castlecove.

eAmon mᴬᶜ ꝣeARAILꞇ
LOS ANGELES 1932
HOP-STEP AND JUMP

Joseph White
All-Ireland Cycling Champion
1952-1953-1954

Above: Retirement, with Cathleen by my side.

Below: RÁS 60 years on: Pete Landy, Sean O'Connor, Pat Healy, Paddy White, Dan Ahern, Arthur Campbell and Eddie Lacey, enjoying the 'men of Rás' reunion in the Sneem Hotel.

Another Title For Cpl. White

CORPORAL PADDY WHITE of the Air Corps C.C., holder of the N.C.A. All-Ireland 100 miles time trial title, returned the fastest time of 64 mins. 31 seconds to win the Tailteann c.c. open 25 miles T.T. held on the out and home course Navan road last evening. He had only 11 seconds to spare over another champion, young Denis O'Connor, of the Harp C.C., who on Tuesday night won the Co. Dublin youth's title.

1. Cpl. P. White (Air Corps), 1 hr. 4 mins. 31 secs.; 2, D. O'Connor (Harp), 1-4-42; 3, F. Ward (Harp), 1-4-44; 4, J. Keogh (Tailteann), 1-4-47; 5, C. O'Reilly (Tailteann), 1-4-48; 6, J. Nolan (Harp), 1-5-9. Team Award: 1, Harp C.C. (O'Connor, Ward, Nolan). Agg. time, 3-14-35; 2, Tailteann (Keogh, O'Reilly, J. Kinnane, 1-7-19). Agg. time 3-16-54. Novice Award: M. Denny (Gate), 1-5-28.

CPL. WHITE AT ENNIS
Consistent C. O'Reilly Is Over-All 'Ras' Leader

From Our Special Representative

ENNIS, Wednesday.

IN a hectic sprint finish along the Limerick Road here this evening 20-years-old Corporal Paddy White, of the Army team, won the fourth stage of Ras Tailteann—Tralee to Ennis. It was a thrilling climax to a great day's race—what a delightful change from the rains and winds of yesterday—as a group of nine battled all out for the verdict.

The lone Antrim rider, Cecil O'Reilly, who has been wonderfully consistent all through, was second, and the Wexford winner, J. O'Brien, third. The first nine, however, were so closely packed at the line that the judges timed them all equally at 4 hrs. 46 mins. 40 secs.

Cpl. White, a native of Cahirdaniel, Co. Kerry, and present holder of the All-Ireland 100 and 50 Miles time trial titles, opened the day in sensational fashion by jumping the field right from the fall of the flag at Castle Street, Tralee.

With him went Paud Fitzgerald, of the Kerry team, and this pair kept forcing the pace faster and faster all day despite a blustery wind.

At Rathluirc, after 62 miles they were joined by O'Reilly, who had put in a sensational solo effort from Listowel. At Limerick — 68 miles, in 3 hrs. 48 mins. 10 secs.—this trio were joined by C. Dunne (Harp), D. Ryan (Limerick), C. Carr (Kildare), J. O'Brien (National), and the Ulster pair, Rogers and Devlin. It was fast and furious over the final 20 miles, until White led out the sprint some 200 yards from the line.

Following his success, White told me: "I never felt better. As the race proceeds I am getting fitter. It was a tough ride, but Paud Fitzgerald gave me great help, and as a time trial specialist, I am eagerly looking forward to to-morrow's run."

As a result of his second place to-day 20-years-old O'Reilly, a bicycle-builder from Belfast, who shared the mountain honours yesterday, regained the yellow jersey he wore into Tralee, which he handed over to Terry Carmody of the Kerry team for to-day's stage.

With an aggregate time of 21hrs. 39 mins. 55 secs, for the four stages, O'Reilly leads by 61 seconds on general classification, from Paddy White, and the "find" of the race, the young Cappamore cyclist, Dennis Ryan, third. White's success to-day has dethroned Kerry from the position as team leaders. Army are now first with National C.C. third.

The new race-leader, O'Reilly, was very emphatic when stating at the finish in his broad Ulster accent: "I never wanted the yellow jersey, as I shall be a marked man to-morrow."

For the Ulster boys it was a highly successful day: O'Reilly, Rogers, from Cookstown, and Seamus Devlin, of Dungannon, rode brilliantly to get into the leading bunch at the finish.

OVER-ALL — Stage 4 (Tralee to Ennis, 119 miles (bonus times 1 min. 45 secs., 30 secs., deducted for first four)—1, Cpl. P. White (Army), 4 hrs. 46 mins 39 secs.; 2, C. O'Reilly (Antrim), 4-46-55; 3, J. O'Brien (National C.C.), 4-46-10; 4, P. Fitzgerald (Kerry), 4-46-35; 5, C. Dunne (Harp), 4-46-40; 6, P. Rogers (Ulster), 4-46-40; equal 7th, D. Ryan (Limerick), C. Carr (Kildare, S. Devlin (Ulster), 4-46-40.

General classification—1, C. O'Reilly (Antrim) 21 hrs. 39 mins. 55 secs.; 2, Cpl. P. White (Army), 21-40-56; 3, D. Ryan (Limerick) 21-41-56; 4, J. O'Brien (National) 21-42-53; 5, C. Dunne (Harp) 21-44-37; 6, P. Rogers (Ulster) 21-46-32.

Team leaders — 1, Army, 66 hrs. 48 mins. 3 secs.; 2, National C.C. 66-58-2.

Prime Winners: Croom — 1, P. White (Army); 2, C. O'Reilly (Antrim); 3, P. Fitzgerald (Kerry). Limerick: Same order.

Pictured at a function in the River Island Hotel, Castleisland, at which presentations were made to Kerry cyclists who won All-Ireland senior championships. A special presentation was made to Patrick Moriarty, from Sneem (seated), who was best Irish rider in this year's FBD Milk Rás. Standing (from left): Dan Ahern, John Mangan (Chairman, Kerry Cycling Board), Johnny Brosnan, Gene Mangan, Pat Healy, Joseph White and Paddy O'Callaghan (Treasurer, Kerry Cycling Board).

National cycling champs honoured in Castleisland

A MOST enjoyable function took place in the River Island Hotel, Castleisland, last Saturday night when, as part of the millennium celebrations, presentations were made by John Mangan, Chairman of the Kerry Cycling Board, to all those Kerrymen who, down through the years, have won All-Ireland senior cycling championships.

The recipients of the presentations were Gene Mangan, Pat Healy, Dan Ahern, John Brosnan, Seamus Kennedy, Patrick Moriarty, Paddy O'Callaghan and Paddy White, known locally as Joe White.

The event was sponsored by Michael O'Donoghue and the River Island Hotel. The beautiful presentations, made locally, were sponsored by Stone Dev Carlow.

A special award was presented to Patrick Moriarty, from Sheen, who was the best Irish rider in this year's FBD Milk Rás.

The function was also used to announce the details of cycling's Millennium Project, which is the construction of a national cycling track in Killorglin. Land was been acquired and plans are being drawn up. It is hoped that planning permission will be in place before the end of the year and that construction will start next spring.

The most beautiful place in the world. Joe White territory.

CHAPTER 15
RING OF KERRY CYCLE RACE
1953

I t came to my notice that there would be a Ring of Kerry cycle race in seven days' time, on a Sunday. Of course, I fancied going down to Killarney by train on Saturday in order to compete.

I stayed at a B&B in Killarney and presented myself on Sunday morning at the starting area. There was a big crowd of cyclists, including, to my surprise, some high-flyers, such as Mick Crystal and his Gate CC teammates, Big Billie O'Brien from Cork, Barney O'Brien from Kildare and other top-notchers. I didn't recognise any of the Kerry cyclists, except for Gene Mangan.

My thinking about the race changed. I had thought that it would be easy, but now I saw that it would be a big challenge.

Before I left Dublin on Saturday, I had readied my bottles to bring to Kerry with me. They contained a special concoction. I also had plenty of liver to eat during the race.

Prior to the start, I had to go to the gents to get rid of excess water. I left my bike, with the bottles fitted, up against a wall. When I came out of the gents, I met my old woodwork teacher, Mr Broadberry, from Waterville Technical School. We had a good chat about the past and he told me that I would have made a good carpenter. We must have spent about 5 minutes talking. He told me that he was well aware of my cycling achievements. He also told me that there was a prime in Kenmare. The first rider to cross a line somewhere in a town or a particular location wins the prime. Oh, my bike! I had forgotten all about it! I experienced a moment of panic, but I found it – not where I left it, though. Strange.

We lined up. A lot of heads were turning to my direction. Half of them had never seen nor heard of me before. Away we went. It took a while to get sorted, but when we did, someone said that the two O'Briens had gone up the road. I know that Barney O'Brien from Kildare was a good climber, as was Willie O'Brien from Cork. If they got to Moll's Gap first, one of them would win the prime in Kenmare. I waited and waited for some move to catch them, but none came. So I had to decide what to do before they were too far ahead.

The road from Killarney to Moll's Gap involved numerous turns, so the two O'Briens were always out of sight. I was getting nervous. I tried to coax some riders into start a chase, but I failed.

"That is it," I said, "here goes."

I attacked and rode strongly up the hill, eventually catching the O'Briens before they got to the top. When I caught up with them, I didn't let up. I passed them to win the first climb in the competition for the King of the Hills, the highest of which was Coomakista. I headed down the hill towards Kenmare and sprinted into the town to win the prime.

We were heading for Sneem and the pace was high. I kept it so, because I wasn't going to let the rest of the bunch catch us. The three of us were about 2 minutes ahead of them. Sneem was quiet, without too many around. We continued on to Castlecove.

"Slow it!" O'Brien from Kildare shouted. "There is a long way to go."

He was feeling the pace, but he stuck in, in fairness to him. We rode through Castlecove, past An Siopa Dubh. There were a few around. We continued on to Bracaragh, where I was born. As we approached, I could see a lot of people around Reens Cross. Did they know that I was in the race? They must have, but they didn't seem to recognise me.

As I approached, I raised my hand and shouted, "Bracaragh!" It was then that the penny dropped. I fell to the rear and as I was passing Michael White's house, I shouted, "Hello, Michael!" An excited dog shot across the road. I just missed him – a lucky escape!

Those at Reens Cross knew now who I was and shouted back, "Joseph, Joseph!" I waved. On to Caherdaniel, which was quiet, and then on to climb Coomakista hill.

"Steady now," I told myself. "Keep a steady pace. It's a tough climb."

When we were halfway up, I knew that O'Brien would attack, so I increased my speed to counter and with about 100 yards to go, I well on my way to winning the second part of the King of the Hills .

Next was Waterville. Time for some liquid. I took a bottle and put it to my mouth – nothing, empty. I threw the bottle away and went for the second bottle – it was empty too. I cursed and cursed. What had happened? The speed down to Waterville was very high. O'Brien from Cork was pushing and I was at the back, confused. I didn't dare try the third bottle at that point as the speed was around 40 mph and it would have been very dangerous. I waited until we reached Waterville. I tried the third bottle. It was empty too! I was so confused. I wouldn't make it without a drink. I needed liquid.

After travelling through Waterville, we reached the next tough climb, outside Waterville. It was during that climb that I realised that I was losing concentration and could barely make the climb to the top.

On we went to Caherciveen. I felt okay again and sprinted through to win the prime. Then I started to lose pace. It was their chance to attack me. I was dropped. Two guys on a motorbike came up beside me.

"Are you okay?" one of them asked.

"No, I have no drink, get me some water."

Between Glenbeigh and Killarney, the two guys on the motorbike arrived with a bottle of water. I gulped it down and swiftly started to recover. I chased the two O'Briens and caught them, but I didn't have the energy to attack them.

I wasn't finished. I had a go for the finish and finished third. It was a close call. A bike's length separated us. It was a big letdown for me, especially when I discovered pinholes in the third bottle. Why would anyone do such a thing?

I got over it though and I must say, apart from the lack of water, I enjoyed the race.

It felt special to race through Bracaragh, Caherdaniel and Castlecove, with memories flashing through my head. I was sad about those people who weren't there to see me: my father, my mother, my brother John and a lot of neighbours – may they rest in peace. But I knew I had done them proud. I had done everyone in South Kerry proud.

CHAPTER 16
100-MILE TIME TRIAL
CHAMPIONSHIP OF IRELAND
1953

In 1952, I had competed in the 100-mile TT all-Ireland and finished in second place – an excellent result considering I was just getting into racing.

Every rider has their own preferences. Some might favour sprinting, short distances, climbing or massed starts. My favourite was time trialling: cycling against the clock over distances from 25 to 100 miles. Time trialling is considered a very tough discipline. It takes concentration, pace, control and determination. I had all of these due to my training regimen and the fact that I trained over long distances on my own.

On the day before the 1953 100-mile TT, I spent a lot of time ensuring that my racing bicycle was in perfect shape, checking the tubulars, the bearings, the positioning, the gears and the selections.

The race would take place on the Navan Road – 50 miles out and 50 miles back. I had trained on this course several times and was very aware of obstacles on the route, such as potholes, turns and rough terrain.

On Saturday evening, I prepared my drink. Three bottles. I also cut fried liver into small pieces. I chewed these during the race, as it was vital to have something in your stomach; otherwise, there was a danger of getting "the knock". The knock is a terrible feeling: all the energy leaves your body and you want to sleep.

I was up at 7 a.m. on Sunday morning. I went for a walk before breakfast, which consisted of a big bowl of porridge and brown bread with jam and milk. No fries for this competitor.

I cycled to Inchicore to go to Mass. I was togged out for the race, so I stayed at the rear of the church. I brought the bicycle into the church for safety reasons. It drew quite a few looks from the parishioners.

After Mass, I drank a bottle of milk and a doughnut-like snack known as a wad. I then proceeded to the start, which was on the Navan Road.

There were a lot of racing cyclists flying up and down the road.

"For what?" I asked myself. "Sure, this is a 100-mile race."

As I was early, I sat down at the side of the road and waited for my turn to start. The space between time trial riders was 2 minutes. For some reason, my name was second last to be called.

"White, to the start line," the starter shouted.

I was nervous and had butterflies in my stomach.

"Five, four, three, two, one ... go!"

I started at an easy pace. There was a long way to go. The weather was blustery, with the odd shower, but nothing to worry about. After about 5 miles, I caught up with the rider who had started before me. I passed him, but didn't utter a word. My speed was around 25 mph. I had settled down and was enjoying myself.

I passed racer after racer. None of them was a top-notcher. I was a bit worried as I didn't know how the top riders were doing. I had some liver and a drink. Coming up to the halfway mark, I saw a rider up front, but try as I might, I couldn't close the gap. Who the hell was he? Suddenly, I realised that he was my friend, the Ghost Rider. He kept putting pressure on me and I had to ride harder and harder to stay with him. As a result, I passed some of the top men. Great! How many more were in front of me? I had a clean road up ahead until I came to the 50-mile turning point. My friend had disappeared.

I turned for home with 50 miles to go and felt that I was in good shape. More liver and drink. I had emptied one bottle, but there were two left and lots of liver. I realised that I had to drink more, so I started taking sups every few miles. I was riding steady and doing around 25 mph. I was catching some of the top riders, which was a great feeling. Then I realised that I was losing concentration. The king of my youth, where I was reared, going to school and especially my parents and brother John, RIP. I slapped my face and legs to wake myself up.

"Wake up!" I shouted to myself.

I was back again. I pedalled hard and began passing the top riders. They had slowed down. I had passed the 60-mile mark.

Oh God, a cramp seized my right leg, which locked up. I couldn't pedal. I braked and fell off the bicycle. I got up and started to walk. A rider flew by without a word. The cramp eased, so I started to run and eventually remounted and started riding again. The cramp had gone, but my leg was sore.

There he was again, teasing me, my friend the Ghost Rider, encouraging me to ride faster and faster. I passed everyone in front of me.

A spectator on a motorcycle came up beside me and shouted, "You are clear, no one up front. Go for it."

I put everything into the last 20 miles. All the liver was gone and all the drink was gone. Would I last? In the distance, I could see the finish. My friend the Ghost Rider reappeared and led me to the finish in sprint mode. Then, he was gone.

"Thanks," I said.

Very few riders completed the course that day. I think that most of them called it a day when I passed them.

I asked a steward what my time had been.

He replied, "Four hours, 5 minutes, 15 seconds. You are the new all-Ireland 100 miles TT champion."

Looking back, I couldn't help but think that if it hadn't been for that cramp, I would have come in under 4 hours, but I had one nonetheless. It was great day to be a Kerryman from Bracaragh, Castlecove.

CHAPTER 17
50-MILE TT ALL-IRELAND
CHAMPIONSHIP 1954

Having been placed in the 50-mile all-Ireland in 1953, I was confident that I could win it in 1954, providing I didn't have any mechanical or health problems. I could not have predicted that it would turn out to be such a frustrating ride. I had overcome intimidation and blocking.

The race would be held in Galway. It was a long distance from my base in Dublin, but I was determined to compete, so I cycled from Dublin to Galway on Thursday.

The race was on Sunday morning. The weather was bad: it was raining and there was a crosswind. As I approached the start, I was told to "F**k off back to Kerry". I was called many names and threatened with physical violence. This made me even more determined. I wasn't going to be intimidated by anyone. I received this kind of treatment at many races, but it didn't trouble me.

West of the Shannon, the Mannions frequently won races. The Mannions were "kings of racing" in the west. My own reputation preceded me and left them hoping that I wouldn't turn up.

Mick Palmer was another regular winner in the west. He was a real sportsman and an excellent bike racer. He had won many races, including All-Irelands.

They found out that I was in town and knew that I posed a danger to them, so they arranged to frustrate and block me to prevent me from winning.

About 5 miles into the race, a car swung out from a side road. I braked and narrowly avoided colliding with it. The car then zig-zagged in front of me so that I couldn't pass. It slowed me down. Two women in the car kept throwing things onto the road. I just kept cycling, despite knowing that I was losing time.

Where was Mannion? He had started the time trial about 10 minutes before me. I was on the lookout for him. It was an out-and-home course, so I should have been able to see him before the turn for home, but I didn't spot him. For about 30 miles, there was no further interference. The car had disappeared and I was really moving, passing racers on the way back. With about 5 miles to go, the blocking started again. At times, I almost had to stop to avoid hitting the car.

At the finish, I learnt that Mannion had achieved the fastest time. His time was 1 hour and 56 minutes, an Irish record. My time was 2 hours and 4 minutes. The president of the National Cycling Association (NCA), Mr Killeen, was at the race. I spoke to him and complained about what had taken place.

He replied, "I was in the car behind you. This will be sorted at the next meeting."

The week after the race, I was called to a top meeting of NCA officials. Mr Mannion and some of his supporters were also at the meeting.

Mr Mannion was called in first. Less than 5 minutes later, he came out and left the hotel. I was called in and told that Mannion had been disqualified for not finishing the distance. He had only completed about 40 miles and hadn't been recorded as having turned at the halfway point. I was now officially the 50-mile time trial champion of Ireland.

What a way to win. I never met Mannion again, even though he had plenty of chances to compete against me.

CHAPTER 18
ALL-ARMY ROAD CYCLING
CHAMPIONSHIP

The All-Army Road Cycling Championship was the first road race organised by the army. It was held in the Curragh of Kildare. The course was a tough one with a hard climb close to the finish. I saw it, this would sort out the sprinters if enough pressure could be applied on this climb.

The army championship trophies were probably the best in the country, so many leading athletes joined the FCA as the FCA were allowed to participate. That weekend would be the busiest in my cycling career as I was competing in three major races. The first race on Friday was the Army Road Cycling Championship, the second race was the Army Track Cycling Championship and on the Sunday I would be defending my status as the 100-mile all-Ireland champion.

On Friday morning, I got ready for the road race and cycled from Baldonnell to the Curragh in good time. I did a few laps of the course and got a feel of the climb. The race started. I was up at the front and had every advantage. The sprinters, as usual, were settled in the bunch, waiting for the finish. But this time they were in a for a big surprise. The distance was 10 miles, which would suit the sprinters. But I was now exceptionally fit and very experienced, so I immediately put on fierce pressure, which resulted in a big line of racers behind me. I kept it going for about 2 miles. When I looked back, I saw that the bunch had split into several groups.

I decided to go hard again for another couple of miles, causing havoc behind me. Only about four riders could keep up with me. Every time we reached the climb, I put on more pressure and opened a big gap between myself and the riders behind. In the form I was in, no one could hold me. I rode strongly to the finish to win the All-Army Road Race Championship. I received a beautiful cup and a winner's medal.

I was happy with my form and was looking forward to the All-Army Track Championship the following day.

I put on my tracksuit and cycled back to Baldonnell. I took care of my bike, as I did after every race, and settled down for a good night's sleep.

CHAPTER 19
ALL-ARMY 3-MILE TRACK CHAMPIONSHIP 1954

Having won the All-Army Road Racing Championship, I was eager to compete in the 3-mile track championship the next day. The first cycling event hadn't taken much out of me as it had only been a 10-mile race.

Getting my racing bike ready was an important part of the process. I had to put on cane wheels and adjust the cycling position. I rode to the Curragh from Baldonnel with two cane wheels up front, held in place by spanners, got to the track in good time, removed the standard wheels and fitted the canes. I was ready and confident.

There would be a lot of track men competing in this race. Some of them were renowned sprinters, but I wasn't worried. Perhaps someone would beat me, but I wouldn't make it easy for them. I was confident and determined. Track racing wasn't my best discipline. I was a road man. In time trialling, I was the best in the country. On the track, I had won the all-Ireland championship in Cork in 1952 and in Tullamore in 1953. Other than those, I hadn't won any other track races. The other riders knew this, so they wouldn't take me seriously on the track – but this would prove to be a big mistake.

A large crowd had assembled from the Southern Command, the Western Command, the Eastern Command, the Curragh Command and from the Air Corps, which I was representing. Each group was supporting their own contestants. There were about twenty riders altogether.

We started slowly, very slowly, standing on pedals, waiting for someone to take the lead. And eventually someone did, but it wasn't me. I held back.

After about a mile, the pace increased. It was getting dangerous at the corners. Everyone was vying for position. The language was choice and there was some elbowing and pushing.

I was still at the back, about 20 yards behind, when an inexperienced rider had a go. This stretched the bunch. I took this as my cue to start moving up towards the front. But not the very front; it was too early. I recognised that the sprinters were still there and I made a calculated decision to attack and put heavy pressure on them. They wouldn't like it, but I was out to win the race.

Over the course of the second mile, I rode hard and stretched them beyond their limits. I was so fit that I remained at the front and left the rest of them about 50 yards behind me. I didn't give up because I knew that there would be an attack and, of course, there was. I was almost caught, but my fitness and determination got me to the finish line first. I had won the All-Army 3-Mile Track Championship.

It was a tough race, but it was worth the effort.

My next challenge was to defend my 100-mile all-Ireland title in Monasterevin the next day.

CHAPTER 20
100-MILE TIME TRIAL
CHAMPIONSHIP OF IRELAND
1954

From 1951 to 1954, I trained hard. I had to or else I may as well have forgotten about cycling. Throughout the winter months of 1953 and 1954, I put in a lot of indoor training, with weights and rollers, and outdoor training, consisting of long distances, road work, mountain climbing and rollers. My weight was at its lowest: I was 10 stone. I had the opportunity to turn professional – either in France or California – but I wanted to win the Rás first.

I had only been racing competitively at the top level for three years and yet I had become the top time-trial racing cyclist. Prior to defending my 100-mile title, I had put in a month of special training – nothing but cycling. I avoided any contact with other cyclists. I was solely absorbed by what lay ahead.

I received invitations to attend dinner dances, club AGMs, etc., but I declined the lot.

The 100-mile race would start in Monasterevin, Co. Kildare. The route would head south for 25 miles, then turn and travel for 50 miles to the Red Cow on the Naas Road, after which cyclists would ride for 25 miles to finish in Monasterevin, Co. Kildare.

The race would start at 10 a.m. on a Sunday morning. There were around thirty riders competing in the race. A 100-mile time trial is a tough race and not everyone fancied travelling that kind of distance against the clock.

I was the defending champion, so I would be the last to start. This gave me an advantage. That Sunday, a steady wind was blowing from the south, which would be of no help during the first 25 miles. It would help during the 50-mile stretch north, but it would be a big problem for the last 25 miles.

Time-trial racing is one of the hardest sporting events. A 100-mile cycle is a huge challenge that requires concentration, the ability to pace oneself, alertness and good nourishment. During training, long distances of over 100 miles must be covered in order to prepare for the race.

At the start, there were around twenty-five riders, but I calculated that only about five, at the most, would pose a challenge. There were 2 minutes between riders starting, so I had to wait for almost an hour before I started as I was the defending champion.

"White next," I heard the starter shout.

My heart gave jumped.

"Deep breath," I said to myself. "This is it, no more time left to dream."

"Five, four, three, two, one, GO!"

I was off, cycling into a fairly stiff breeze.

"Steady," I said to myself, "you have 100 miles to go. Pace yourself."

I settled down into my favourite time-trial mode. The wind was a bit of a problem. I knew at that early stage that my overall time would be over 4 hours. But I was determined to win. Over the course of about the first 10 miles, I passed some of my competitors, including that great Kildare racing cyclist from Monasterevin, Con Carr. As I passed him, I heard him say, "For fuck's sake, White, give me a chance!"

Catching up with and passing Con was enormous encouraging as he was good at time trialling and had won many races. I pressed on, though the headwind resulted in me making slower progress than usual over the first 25 miles. However, I kept calm and concentrated and passing other competitors made me feel good.

I reached the turn, 25 miles out, after around 1 hour and 5 minutes. I would have the wind at my back for the 50 miles back to the Red Cow, near Dublin city. I went into top gear, drank some liquid and ate some liver. Suddenly, I felt a shudder – the chain had jumped the chain wheel. Should I stop? No, I assessed what had happened and was able to bend down and get the chain back onto the chain wheel. I was okay again.

"Don't put too much pressure on," I told myself. "Just increase speed gradually."

This worked. I was travelling at around 35 mph, sometimes hitting 40 mph, which allowed me to make up time that I had lost during the first 25 miles.

I was lucky to have escaped a few potholes and avoided getting any punctures. I was comfortable and wasn't overdoing it. More drink, more liver. By the time I had covered around 70 miles, I had recovered the lost time and doing well. But I knew that I would have to cycle the last 25 miles into the wind. At this stage, I had passed every cyclist still in the race who had started before me. Normally, this would indicate that I was sure to win the race, as long as I didn't have an accident. However, I was determined to drive to the end. I had one bottle of fluid left and a few pieces of liver. I had to decide whether I should drink all that remained in the bottle and eat the rest of the liver or ration them out. I decided to drink the lot, discard the bottles, eat the liver and hope for the best.

I turned into the headwind for the last 25 miles. I had thought that there was no one up ahead, but I was wrong. There he was, about 100 yards in front of me. I tried to catch him, but he kept the distance. I rode as fast as I could. This went on for about 20 miles. I was nearing exhaustion, but still this guy kept his lead. Of course it was my old friend, the Ghost Rider.

Travelling through open countryside of the Curragh, I had no protection from the wind. It was hard going. As I cycled through Kildare town, I was recognised and received great encouragement.

"Up the kingdom! Go for it, Paddy."

"Up, up, Paddy."

This gave me a new lease of life and I went all out for the last few miles. My body ached, my wrists were sore, my lower back was in pain and I had lost some of the power in my legs. I reached Monasterevin. Where was the finish line? There it was. I crossed it and rode on for about a mile as a warm-down before returning to the start. I put one leg on the road and collapsed. I could not stand.

I was helped to the footpath. I asked for a bottle of milk and a wad. Slowly, I recovered and was able to stand up. The president of the NCA and others were in a huddle at the start line. When they had finished deliberating, the president came across the road, put his arm around me and said, "Paddy, you done a wonderful ride. We can't believe you done such a time. It was under 4 hours, a world record. But we have to check the distance again and we will let you know the exact time."

I burst out crying. The pressure was off. I thought of my mother, my father and my brother John – may they rest in peace. They were looking down on me and I am sure they were very proud. I thought of my home in Bracaragh, the people of Castlecove, Caherdaniel, who would share in the glory of this achievement.

A week later, it was confirmed that the distance was 100 miles and that my time had been 3 hours, 58 minutes and 15 seconds. It was a world record. My average speed had been 25 mph+.

I felt so proud to be from Bracaragh, Castlecove – a Kerryman.

After a while, I put on my tracksuit and cycled back to the Air Corps Camp in Baldonnel. I was exhausted. After a light meal, I went to bed and slept until noon the following day. Word got out about the ride I had put in; it was the talk of cycling circles. Yes, I had made history, but I hadn't set out to ride the fastest 100 miles – it had happened because I was extremely fit and determined to defend my all-Ireland title. Thanks, Ghost Rider.

When I recovered from the 100-mile race, I started getting ready for the eight-day Rás. I was fiercely determined to win it.

Even though my favourite racing was time trialling, I was able to match anyone in hill climbing and massed-start racing.

One race I had to compete in was the 25 Miles TT All-Ireland Championship. This race was held in Cork. In order to win the All-Round Championship of Ireland, I had to finish at least in at least third position.

A Cork cyclist, Tom Lavin , was the favourite to win. Could I beat him? Well, I didn't manage to beat him on the day. I finished in third place. I had some mechanical trouble at about the 15-mile mark, but even if I hadn't, I'm sure Tom would still have won. Nevertheless, as I had come third, I won the All-Round Championship of Ireland.

CHAPTER 21
THE RÁS 1954: EIGHT-DAY
RACE AROUND IRELAND

My training during 1953/1954 was geared towards a number of races, with specific goals in mind. These goals were:

- to win the Rás 8 Day Cycle Race;
- to defend my 100-miles time trial win;
- to win the All-Army Championships;
- to defend my All-Round Championship;
- to win the 50-Miles TT Championship;
- to win the All-Round Championship.

As well as the above, I competed in several massed-start and time-trial races, with some success, especially in the time trials, in which I was practically unbeatable. Being a time triallist was special. It was hard going whatever the distance, but over distances of 25 miles, 50 miles and 100 miles, I was unbeatable in 1954.

Having achieved the all-Army road and track races and the 50-mile All-Ireland, I was ready for the Rás. I was probably more ready than most racers, as I trained so hard and gave up so much. In fact, the training was harder than the racing. Yes, I was fit and focused on winning the Rás.

With the Rás in my sights and all my previous successes under my belt, I had decided to turn professional and had made contacts in both France and the USA – but I had to win the Rás first.

CHAPTER 22
THE FIRST STAGE OF THE RÁS: DUBLIN TO WEXFORD

What a day. There was a strong wind and rain from the south.

The crowd at the GPO was huge. Thousands of spectators had gathered for the start of the race. I and my army teammates were amongst the starters. There wasn't much conversation as everyone was tense and nervous. The race started at the GPO, but was neutralised until it reached the turn-off into Clondalkin, when the flag was dropped and we were on our way.

I was up front and cycling into the wind and the rain, like everyone else, but when I had travelled a mile, I attacked and opened a big gap. At Newlands Cross, I was 30 seconds clear and gaining time. The race had only started and I was away on my own – crazy stuff. At Naas, I was caught by three riders who had escaped the pack. All four of us worked together to increase our lead by over 1 minute.

At Kildare, we were 2 minutes ahead. I was feeling relaxed, but the rain and the wind were tough to bear. We continued on through Carlow and into Enniscorthy, riding hard and still gaining time on the pack. Wexford was getting near and we were conscious of each other for a stage win.

Suddenly, my rear wheel started to shake. I had a puncture. No need to panic. I had a spare tubular over my shoulder. I got off the bicycle, released the back wheel and pulled off the tubular, which had been punctured by the wheel rim. The rain got at the exposed rim and no matter how hard I tried to get it on, it wouldn't stick. The rim was too wet.

I took off my jersey and tried to dry rim. This seemed to do the trick. I had a new tubular on and managed to inflate it. I could see that the tubular wouldn't stay on long, but I got back on the bike nonetheless and rode carefully towards Wexford.

Before reaching Wexford, I was overtaken by the pack. I finished well after the winner, who had been a fellow member of the original breakaway.

Soaking wet and disappointed, I went to my accommodation, had something to eat and went to bed cursing my bad luck. Ah well, there were another seven days to go. I wasn't finished yet.

CHAPTER 23
THE SECOND STAGE OF THE RÁS: WEXFORD TO CORK

Prior to the start of Stage 2, I watched the president of the NCA put the yellow jersey on Joe O'Brien, who had won the first stage. It was hard to take. I knew that I could have won the first stage. I was also disappointed because I had lost a lot of time. I estimated that I had lost about 10 minutes on the leader during Stage 1.

I was still convinced that I could win the Rás, but I knew that I would have to attack non-stop. I started Stage 2 and immediately attacked, splitting the bunch into segments. I had created mayhem and now I was away with about twelve other riders.

The pace was very high for about 50 miles, then it settled down, but any slowing down was not to my liking. I attacked and increased the speed again. I won several primes along the route, but I didn't win any prizes until we were approaching Cork city.

At Watergrasshill, I attacked and only five riders stayed with me. I had a problem changing gears and could not get into top gear. This cost me and I only finished third into Cork.

At the end of Stage 2, I had recovered several minutes of lost time and now was only 5 minutes behind the leader, O'Reilly from Antrim. I had recovered from the disaster of Stage 1.

Chapter 24
The Third Stage of the Rás: Cork to Tralee

During this stage, the climb up to Moll's Gap would decide who could finish well up the field. Early on, the pace was normal, except for one attack that did not develop. All the riders had Moll's Gap in mind. Everyone knew that it would separate the men from the boys and it sure did. On the climb, I was very comfortable and was able to contain any breaks. About ten riders climbed, having dropped everyone else. I attacked and got away, heading for the top by myself.

As bad luck would have it, my chain broke about 100 yards from the top. I was in shock. What would I do? Run like hell with the bike on my back to try and get to the top first? But no, I was left sitting at the side of the road, without a bike, losing time again. Thankfully, I had a bit of luck. Our team car arrived and I was given a spare bicycle to cycle like hell down into Killarney and on to Tralee, about 4 minutes behind the winner, Terry Carmody of Kerry.

I would have to try again and make up the time somehow. There were five stages to go and the opposition was getting tired, whereas I felt that I was getting stronger. I had a chance.

I stayed with my cousins in Tralee and had a good rest and a hearty breakfast the next morning.

CHAPTER 25
THE FOURTH STAGE OF THE RÁS: TRALEE TO ENNIS

After my stay in Tralee, I was ready for the race from Tralee to Ennis, which covered a distance of 110 miles. I was positioned up at the front and got into the action as soon as the starter dropped the flag. I rode fairly strongly at the front. After about 5 miles, I looked back to find, to my surprise, that I had broken away from the bunch, but one rider had kept up with me. I had never seen him before. He was powerful-looking racer who had a big smile on his face every time I looked back at him. I kept up the pace and was increasing the distance between myself and the bunch all the time.

The guy who had kept up with me shot past me. I had a job to catch him. When I did, I told him to steady up as there was a long way to go and that, in future, when he was coming up to do his bit, not to sprint, but to gradually increase speed until he got to the front.

He asked me if I was Paddy White. I said, "Yes, who are you?"

"Paudie," he said.

"Are you a Corkman?" I asked.

"Jesus, no," he said. "How far ahead are we?"

"About 5 miles," I said. "Ride steady."

And we did ride steady. Coming up to the 60-mile mark, a motorcyclist came up and told us that a chase was approaching fast.

"Who are they?" I asked.

"O'Reilly, O'Brien, Dunne, Rogers and Crowe."

"Crowe!" I shouted. "For fuck's sake, he is my teammate. What is he doing chasing me?"

I was mad as hell. Imagine my own teammate helping the others to catch me.

However, we rode until we were caught just before Limerick. There was a prime in the city with a massive cup for the winner. I looked at those around me and decided that I was going to have a go at winning the prime. I succeeded, beating O'Reilly, and Paudie came in third position. We continued over Limerick Bridge and on to Ennis. The pace was very fast as the bunch was in disarray and well back, so the changes of moving up on general classification was in my mind and so I pushed and pushed until outside Ennis. I slipped back a bit. O'Reilly and O'Brien were in front of me. Now it was time to act. I put everything into a mighty sprint to gradually haul in O'Brien and then O'Reilly. I won by inches.

The bunch was well back. I had made up a lot of time. I was less than 1 minute behind the Rás leader, O'Reilly. O'Brien, who would ultimately win the Rás, was 2 minutes behind. Stage 5 would take place in two parts. The first part was a time trial, my favourite event.

There was ceili in Ennis, but I went to bed early – the following day's race was important.

CHAPTER 26
THE FIFTH STAGE OF THE RÁS:
ENNIS TO GALWAY

Thanks to my victory the previous day, I was only 1 minute behind the leader. I was on track to win the Rás. Those other riders who were still in the Rás were feeling the strain after four hard days in the saddle.

As I had won the all-Ireland 100-miles and 50-mile time trials and set a world record, I was a clear favourite to win this stage. As the 100-Mile Time Trial Irish Champion, I was honoured to be the last to start – what a break!

I warmed up by riding slowly for about the first 3 miles and then I upped the pace, got into time trial mode and concentrated. I was really moving, passing rider after rider, but most importantly, I flew past the race leader. Now I was in the lead and gaining time. I was really comfortable and even though I was travelling at around 28 miles per hour, I was not yet cycling at full speed.

On a long stretch of road, I saw a policeman standing under a bridge up ahead. The bridge was over an S-bend in the road. As I approached, I gestured to make sure that the road was clear ahead. He beckoned me on and I cut in close on the wrong side of the road to gain time.

All I remember is getting up off the road and looking for my bicycle, which was in the ditch. There was blood everywhere. My right leg was bleeding heavily from where the handlebar of my bike had ripped a deep gash in my thigh. I had two broken ribs on my right side and one of the spokes from the front wheel had penetrated my right hand. I had a wound on the right side of my head, my shoulder hurt and my body was covered in countless scratches and grazes. The bicycle was also in bad shape. The gear selection was all messed up. The handlebars were turned and so was the saddle. What a disaster.

I was dazed, but I did my best to get the bike into shape.

The driver of the car was also in shock. I told him that it was my fault because I had taken a chance.

I rode into Galway and even though I had lost a huge amount of time, I was still within striking distance of the new leader, Joe O'Brien from Dublin.

I tried to start next day, but I had too many injuries and decided to give up.

As a result of that crash, I lost the power in my right leg and never competed in another cycle race.

I was finished.

CHAPTER 27
ACHIEVEMENTS

All-Ireland Titles

Road and Track All-Ireland Championships	13
All-Army Championships	2
Command Championships	4
Tóstal Championships	2
Stage 4 of An Rás 1954	1
CPs (Competitor-Paced)	2
Dublin Omagh	1
Tour of Mayo	3rd
Tour of Dublin	1
Tour of Kildare	1
Ring of Kerry	3rd
Cork Around the Houses	1

As well as the championship wins, I won numerous other races. I also lost quite a few.

I also achieved a time-trial world record in 1954. I completed 100 miles in 3 hours, 58 minutes and 16 seconds. This made me the first cyclist in the world to complete 100 miles in under 4 hours. To this day, there is no evidence that anyone has bettered this time on a bicycle.

CHAPTER 28
THAT 100-MILE TIME TRIAL WORLD RECORD

In 1954, I cycled a 100-mile time trial in a time of 3 hours, 58 minutes and 16 seconds. In 1956, a British cyclist by the name of Ray Booty also broke the 100-mile barrier. His time was 3 hours, 58 minutes and 28 seconds. Both times broke the 100-mile time trial barrier, but under different circumstances.

I competed under rules of the NCA (National Cycling Association), which recognised the thirty-two counties as Irish, so the NCA was not recognised by the international cycling body of which England was a member. When Ray Booty broke the 100-mile barrier, the intention was to claim that this was a world record, but word was already out that an Irishman had cycled the 100 miles in less than 4 hours in 1954.

In 2017, a chance meeting took place in London when I was visiting my brother, Michael, who was sick in hospital. I met some of his workmates at his bedside. As we were talking, one of his friends, Gerry Fox, said to me, "I believe you were a cyclist – your brother mentioned it."

I said that I had been. He said that he had been a member of the same club as Roy Booty. He had been present when Booty rode the 100 miles on the Bath Road.

I immediately said, "Yes, his time was 3 hours, 58 minutes, 28 seconds."

He looked at me and said, "Was it you?"

"Yes," I said, "I rode the 100 in 1954: 3 hours, 58 minutes, 16 seconds – 32 seconds faster than Booty."

He put his hand out to me and said, "I know why your record wasn't recognised. It was political. My parents are Irish. I can't believe what I have just heard."

During my cycling days, I became a good friend of a cyclist named Denis O'Connor and we raced against each other many times. A letter he wrote to me in 2012 included a cutting from The Evening Press, dated 10 August 1956, which highlighted Booty's achievement. But Denis O'Connor added a note to the cutting indicating that I had been the first cyclist in the world to break the 100 miles TT in 1954.

CHAPTER 29
RELATED EVENTS

In 1947, the UCI (Union Cycliste International) indicated that the NCA (National Cycling Association) must confine its area of activity to the twenty-six counties of the Republic. The NCA, a thirty-two-county body, refused and was therefore expelled from the UCI.

In 1949, a number of Irish clubs broke away from the NCA and formed a new association that recognised the twenty-six counties. It called itself Cumann Rothaíochta na hÉireann (CRE). This organisation obtained international recognition from the UCI. Nevertheless, from 1953 to 1973, the Rás was run by the NCA.

In 1974, a number of cycling associations got together in order to unify cycling in Ireland. In 1978, the Irish Cycling Tripartite Committee (ICTC) was formed. Consequently, Irish cycling became united and was administered by the ICTC. This body was recognised by the UCI. Proper records were, in many cases, lost as a result of the changeover. Photographs were also lost, besides which a photographer would not have been available most of the time.

There was serious rivalry between the NCA and the CRE. To put it bluntly, they hated each other. I was the victim of such rivalry on a number of occasions between 1950 and 1954.

I was a member of the thirty-two-county NCA. I used to train solo and, on one occasion, whilst training in the Wicklow Mountains, I met another cyclist who was also out training on his own. Without any knowledge of each other's politics or affiliations, we became cycling friends and agreed to train together. It turned out that this cyclist was none other than the great Shay Elliot, who eventually turned professional and made a name for himself in the Tour de France. He was a member of CRE. He was the top cyclist in the CRE and I was the top cyclist in the NCA. This didn't trouble either of us – we were sportsmen. I was invited to a dinner dance promoted by the CRE and I decided to go. I was presented with a plaque as recognition of my status within the NCA. However, word got out that I had attended the function, which, in the eyes of the NCA executive, was a mortal sin. I was called to a meeting to explain my actions and was told that I might never cycle again if I ever attended or mixed with the CRE again. There are several other such episodes I could relate that illustrate the tension between the two organisations.

Other great Irish cyclists who left the NCA to achieve international recognition included Carl McCarthy and John Lackey, who proved themselves capable of matching the best in international competitions. I competed against both of them when they were members of the NCA.

CHAPTER 30
THE IRON MAN

Mike "Iron Man" Murphy was born in Caherciveen, Co. Kerry, in 1934. In his early youth, he took part in athletic activities such as weight lifting, body building, circus acts and so on. Consequently, he developed immense body strength. He was involved in all kinds of sport throughout his life and was especially keen on cycling. He won the Eight-Day Rás Tailteann in 1958. I got to know Mike many years later and it was through this friendship that we learnt more about each other's involvement in cycling.

On our very first meeting, he greeted me as his idol.

"It was you who got me involved in cycling," he said. "I saw you racing through Cahirciveen."

I was surprised and honoured by his remarks.

Every time I visited my old home in Bracaragh, I would call Mike to chat about cycling. His knowledge of sport, international affairs, places and people astounded me. I called to visit him once with two of my granddaughters. They were home on holidays from New Zealand. Well, he started talking about New Zealand and he wouldn't stop for about an hour. My granddaughters were amazed by his knowledge.

Mike Murphy was, to me, a very sincere person who had had a tough life as a child, but was happy with his lot. I respected him for what he had achieved in cycling.

Mike was a good friend to me and a man whom I respected very much. He was a legend in cycling, but, in my opinion, he was a legend in other areas too.

Many stories are told about Mike and while many are true, many others do not have any foundation.

Conclusion

I am privileged to be able to record some of my sporting achievements, especially in bicycle racing, my achievements in which exceeded my wildest dreams. After all, I was only lad from Bracaragh, Castlecove, Co. Kerry, who landed in Dublin with two and six in his pocket.

As well as cycle racing, I also honoured by Dublin GAA for my contribution to training members of the Dublin team from 1950 to 1960.

I also contributed to the community of Swords and I was chairman of the local council and chairman of the Fingallians GAA Club.

I thank all those who supported me during my cycle racing years, especially the Irish Air Corps at Baldonnel.

My cycling career may have finished with a serious crash during Stage 5 of the Rás in 1954, but such is sport. You can be lucky and you can be unlucky. I want to say thank you to Weeshie Fogarty, who brought many of my triumphs to light. May he rest in peace.

To the people of Castlecove, Bracaragh and Caherdaniel, I trust that I have done you proud. Being from that locality was special. I never forgot where I came from. Indeed, to this day, I consider it a privilege to be a Kerryman.

To Brendan and Carmel Galvin, from An Siopa Dubh, thanks for your kindness to me. You are a special presence in Castlecove. Seeing all the photographs displayed in your bar fills me with pride because so many people from the area became famous, be it in sport or other areas – thank you.

To conclude, I dedicate this book to my family and wish for the money raised by this book to be given to the Caherciveen Hospice.

Finally, the Ghost Rider…
Yes, he was there when I needed him – we never spoke, even
though he annoyed me at times.

Postscript
Who was the Ghost Rider?

During my youth around Reems Cross I listened to many stories about ghosts, the banshee, people coming back from the dead. In one case, a cattle dealer who bought a cow from my uncle swore on his deathbed he would come back to haunt the Whites. My uncle had omitted to give him any 'luck money' when he bought the cow. The amount would have been one shilling at the time.

Stories were told about the ghost of the dealer, who used to bang on my uncle's roof at night and even caused the death of some of his cattle. The family certainly suffered at his hand. Eventually he was convinced to stop frightening the family and he did.

In my cycling days, however, the ghost came back. He would appear about 20 yards in front of me during races, and would encourage me to greater efforts, to win races that I couldn't have otherwise. He was friendly and helpful, and it was hard to imagine that he was the same ghost as before. When I told my story to some of the locals, however, they believed it was certainly him, and that he had been instructed to help me by St Peter if he was ever going to get into heaven.

There are other ghosts in Reems Cross, of course. There is the ghost that was seen putting stones into a Seine boat at the pier in Castlecove by night, and the two mules who passed silently along the road, each carrying a ghost on its back. But that's another story.